Town Mouse and Country Mouse

Retold by Annette Smith
Illustrated by Betty Greenhatch

NELSON PRICE MILBURN

Once upon a time,
there was a little grey mouse
who lived in a very big house
in town.

One morning, he said,
"I need a holiday.
I will go and visit my cousin
in the country."

Off he went.
At last, he reached his cousin's home
in a cornfield.

"Come in. Come in," said Country Mouse.
"I am pleased to see you.
You are just in time
to have supper with me."

Town Mouse was feeling very hungry
after his long walk.
He looked at the food
that Country Mouse had spread out.

"Is that all you have to eat?"
said Town Mouse.

"You can have this slice of apple,"
said Country Mouse,
"and we can share
the peas and the corn."

After supper, Town Mouse tried to sleep
on the bed of straw
that Country Mouse had made for him.

He thought about his own bed
of soft warm feathers
back at the big house.

Town Mouse tossed and turned.
It was so quiet in the country.
But what was that strange noise?
An owl swooped down
over the cornfield.

"Tu-whit! Tu-whoo!" it cried
as it flew on.

Town Mouse shivered with fear.

Next morning, Country Mouse said, "Let me show you around the cornfield."

No sooner had they begun their walk when a large weasel rushed by.

The two little mice hid among the cornstalks.

Town Mouse was very frightened.

"I don't like it here in the country," he said. "Why don't you come and stay with me? You will have plenty to eat and a soft feather bed to sleep on."

"Yes, I would like that," said Country Mouse.

Town Mouse and Country Mouse set off.

It was getting dark
as they made their way
along the busy streets.

The bright lights and tramping feet
frightened Country Mouse.

At last, they reached the big house
where Town Mouse lived.

Country Mouse followed Town Mouse down a long passageway, under a door, and into the kitchen.

Country Mouse could smell
something delicious and he began
to feel better at once.

He climbed onto the table with Town Mouse,
and there before him was so much food
that he felt very excited.
He had just started to nibble
some tasty cheese
when the door opened
and in came the cook.

"Quick! Hide!" whispered Town Mouse as he dashed for safety.
CRASH! BANG!
The cook rattled some pots and pans.
"Mice!" she said.
"Mice have been eating the cheese! I am going to have to set a trap."

Country Mouse crouched behind a jug.

When the cook had gone,
Country Mouse looked around
for his cousin.
He couldn't see him anywhere.
But there, asleep by the fire,
was an enormous cat.

Where, oh where was Town Mouse?

Then he heard a loud whisper.
"Over here! Quick!"
It was Town Mouse calling to him.
Country Mouse raced down
the leg of the table
and across the kitchen floor
to the hole in the wall.

"Don't worry," laughed Town Mouse.
"We can have some more food tomorrow.
There's always plenty left over
for us to eat. Come along.
You can have my soft feather bed."

But Country Mouse could not sleep.
He lay awake all night.
He could hear the big cat
meowing and scratching
at the mouse hole.
He could hear the tramping of feet
and the sound of loud voices.

In the morning, Country Mouse said,
"It is time for me to go home."

"But there is so much to see here,"
said Town Mouse.
"I want to show you the town."

"No, thank you!" said Country Mouse.
"The town is no place for me,
and the country is no place for you."

And he ran off down the road
back to his home in the cornfield.

A play
Town Mouse
and
Country Mouse

People in the play

Reader

Once upon a time,
there was a little grey mouse
who lived in a very big house in town.

Town Mouse

I need a holiday.
I will go and visit my cousin
in the country.

Reader

At last, he reached his cousin's home
in a cornfield.

Country Mouse

Come in! Come in!
I am so pleased to see you.
You are just in time
to have supper with me.

Town Mouse

I have had a long walk
and I am feeling very tired and hungry.

Reader

Town Mouse looked at the food
that Country Mouse had spread out.

Town Mouse

That's not very much food.
Is that all you have to eat?

Country Mouse

You can have this slice of apple,
and we can share
the peas and the corn.
When we have finished our supper,
I will make a bed for you.

Reader
Town Mouse tossed and turned
on the bed of straw
that Country Mouse had made for him.

Town Mouse
Oh, how I wish that I was back
at the big house in my own bed
of soft warm feathers.
This bed is so hard.
I cannot sleep. It's so quiet here, too.

Reader
Just then, an owl swooped down
over the cornfield.

Owl
Tu-whit! Tu-whoo!

Town Mouse (shivering with fear)
What's that noise? It's so scary.
I don't like this place at all.

Reader
The next morning, Country Mouse took Town Mouse out for a walk.

Country Mouse
Let me show you around the cornfield. There's lots to see.

Reader
No sooner had they begun their walk when a large weasel rushed by.

Town Mouse
What's that? What's that?

Country Mouse
Quick! Hide! It's a weasel. They eat mice.

Town Mouse
I don't like it here in the country.
There are strange noises
and scary animals.
Why don't you come and stay with me?
You will have plenty to eat
and a soft feather bed to sleep on.

Country Mouse
Yes, I would like that.
I will come with you to the town.

Reader
It was getting dark
as Town Mouse and Country Mouse
reached the town.

Country Mouse

It's so busy here,
and there is so much noise
and so many bright lights.

Town Mouse

Don't be scared.
We're here now. This is my home.
Follow me down this passageway,
then we'll squeeze under the door
and go into the kitchen.

Reader

Country Mouse scuttled quickly along
behind Town Mouse.

Country Mouse

I can smell something good to eat.
I feel much better already.

Town Mouse

Climb up here onto the table, cousin.
Look at all this food!

Country Mouse

I've never seen so much food before.
This cheese is so tasty.

Reader

Just then, the kitchen door opened
and in came the cook
with a crash and a bang.

Town Mouse

Quick! Hide! The cook will see you!

Country Mouse

Where do I hide?
I know, I can get behind this jug.

Cook (banging some pots and pans)
Mice!
Mice have been eating the cheese!
I am going to have to set
a trap to catch them.

Reader
At last, the cook stomped out.

Country Mouse
Thank goodness she's gone! I'm so scared.
I have to find Town Mouse.
Where, oh where is he? Oh, no!
There's an enormous cat by the fire.
I hope it doesn't wake up.
Where is Town Mouse?

Town Mouse (whispering)
Country Mouse, I'm over here.
Come on! Quick! Run!

Reader
Country Mouse raced down
the leg of the table
and across the kitchen floor
to the hole in the wall.

Country Mouse
I'm so glad to find you again.

Town Mouse (laughing)
Don't worry.
We can have some more food tomorrow.
There's always plenty left over
for us to eat.
Come along.
You can have my soft feather bed.

Country Mouse

I can't sleep here in this big house.
There are lots of loud noises
and so many tramping feet.

Cat

Meow! I smell mice in here. Meow!

Country Mouse

That cat has been scratching
at the hole in this wall all night.
I'm really scared of it.
I'm going home in the morning.
I don't like it here.

Reader

The next morning, Town Mouse
was ready to show Country Mouse
the town.

Town Mouse

Come on, cousin. There's so much
to see here in the town.
I want to show you around.

Country Mouse

No, thank you!
The town is no place for me,
and the country is no place for you.
I am a country mouse
and you are a town mouse.

Reader

And Country Mouse waved goodbye
to his cousin and ran off
down the road
back to his home in the cornfield.